THE MERCHANT OF VENICE

WILLIAM SHAKESPEARE

DRAMATIS PERSONAE.

AS FIRST PERFORMED, SATURDAY, JUNE 12, 1858.

DUKE OF VENICE Mr. H. MELLON.

PRINCE OF MOROCCO (Suitors to Portia)

PRINCE OF ARRAGON Mr. RAYMOND.

ANTONIO (the Merchant of Venice)

BASSANIO (his Friend)

SALANIO (Friends to Antonio and Bassanio)

SALARINO Mr. G. EVERETT.

GRATIANO Mr. WALTER LACY.

LORENZO (in love with Jessica)

SHYLOCK (a Jew)

TUBAL (a Jew, his Friend)

LAUNCELOT GOBBO (a Clown, servant to Shylock)

OLD GOBBO (Father to Launcelot)

LEONARDO (Servants to Bassanio)

STEPHANO

BALTHAZAR (Servant to Portia) .

HERALD

PORTIA (a rich Heiress).

NELISSA (her Waiting Maid)

JESSICA (Daughter to Shylock)

Magnificoes of Venice, Officers of the Court of Justice, Gaoler, Servants, and other Attendants.

ACT I.

SCENE I.—VENICE. SAINT MARK'S PLACE.

Various groups of Nobles, Citizens, Merchants, Foreigners, Water-Carriers, Flower Girls, &c., pass and repass. Procession of the Doge, in state, across the square.

ANTONIO, SALARINO, and SALANIO come forward.

Ant. In sooth, I know not why I am so sad;

It wearies me; you say, it wearies you;

But how I caught it, found it, or came by it,

What stuff 'tis made of, whereof it is born,

I am to learn;

And such a want-wit sadness makes of me,

That I have much ado to know myself.

Salar. Your mind is tossing on the ocean;

There, where your argosies with portly sail,

Like signiors and rich burghers on the flood,

Do overpeer the petty traffickers,

That curt'sy to them, do them reverence,

As they fly by them with their woven wings.

Sal. Believe me, Sir, had I such venture forth,

The better part of my affections would
Be with my hopes abroad. I should be still
Plucking the grass, to know where sits the wind;
Peering in maps, for ports, and piers, and roads;
And every object that might make me fear
Misfortune to my ventures, out of doubt,
Would make me sad.

Salar. My wind, cooling my broth,
Would blow me to an ague, when I thought
What harm a wind too great might do at sea.
I should not see the sandy hour-glass run,
But I should think of shallows and of flats;
And see my wealthy Andrew dock'd in sand,
Vailing her high-top lower than her ribs,
To kiss her burial.
Shall I have the thought
To think on this? and shall I lack the thought
That such a thing, bechanc'd, would make me sad?
But tell not me; I know Antonio
Is sad to think upon his merchandize.

Ant. Believe me, no: I thank my fortune for it,
My ventures are not in one bottom trusted,
Nor to one place; nor is my whole estate
Upon the fortune of this present year:
Therefore my merchandize makes me not sad.

Salar. Why, then, you are in love.

Ant. Fie, fie!

Salar. Not in love, neither? Then let us say you are sad,

Because you are not merry: an 'twere as easy

For you to laugh and leap, and say you are merry,

Because you are not sad.

Sal. Here comes Bassanio, your most noble kinsman,

Gratiano, and Lorenzo: Fare you well;

We leave you now with better company.

Salar. I would have staid till I had made you merry,

If worthier friends had not prevented me.

Ant. Your worth is very dear in my regard.

I take it your own business calls on you,

And you embrace the occasion to depart.

Enter BASSANIO, LORENZO, and GRATIANO.

Salar. Good morrow, my good lords.

Bas. Good signiors, both, when shall we laugh? Say, when?

You grow exceeding strange: Must it be so?

Salar. We'll make our leisures to attend on yours.

Exeunt SALARINO and SALANIO.

Lor. My lord Bassanio, since you have found Antonio,

We two will leave you; but at dinner-time

I pray you have in mind where we must meet.

Bas. I will not fail you.

Gra. You look not well, Signor Antonio;

You have too much respect upon the world:

They lose it that do buy it with much care.

Believe me, you are marvellously chang'd.

Ant. I hold the world but as the world, Gratiano;

A stage, where every man must play a part,

And mine a sad one.

Gra. Let me play the fool:

With mirth and laughter let old wrinkles come;

And let my liver rather heat with wine,

Than my heart cool with mortifying groans.

Why should a man, whose blood is warm within,

Sit like his grandsire, cut in alabaster?

Sleep when he wakes? and creep into the jaundice

By being peevish? I tell thee what, Antonio,

I love thee, and it is my love that speaks;—

There are a sort of men, whose visages

Do cream and mantle like a standing pond:

And do a wilful stillness entertain,

With purpose to be dress'd in an opinion

Of wisdom, gravity, profound conceit;

As who should say, 'I am Sir Oracle,

And when I ope my lips let no dog bark!'

O, my Antonio, I do know of these,

That therefore only are reputed wise

For saying nothing; when I am very sure,

If they should speak, 'twould almost damn those ears

Which, hearing them, would call their brothers fools.

I'll tell thee more of this another time:

But fish not with this melancholy bait,

For this fool gudgeon, this opinion.

Come, good Lorenzo:—Fare ye well, a while;

I'll end my exhortation after dinner.

Lor. Well, we will leave you, then, till dinner-time:

I must be one of these same dumb wise men,

For Gratiano never lets me speak.

Gra. Well, keep me company but two years more,

Thou shalt not know the sound of thine own tongue.

Ant. Farewell: I'll grow a talker for this gear.

Gra. Thanks, i'faith; for silence is only commendable

In a neat's tongue dried, and a maid not vendible.

Exeunt GRATIANO and LORENZO.

Ant. Is that any thing now?

Bas. Gratiano speaks an infinite deal of nothing, more than any man in all Venice. His reasons are as two grains of wheat hid in two bushels of chaff; you shall seek all day ere you find them; and when you have them they are not worth the search.

Ant. Well; tell me now, what lady is the same

To whom you swore a secret pilgrimage,

That you to-day promis'd to tell me of?

Bas. 'Tis not unknown to you, Antonio,

How much I have disabled mine estate,

By something showing a more swelling port

Than my faint means would grant continuance.

To you, Antonio, I owe the most in money and in love;

And from your love I have a warranty

To unburthen all my plots and purposes,

How to get clear of all the debts I owe.

Ant. I pray you, good Bassanio, let me know it;

And, if it stand, as you yourself still do,

Within the eye of honour, be assur'd

My purse, my person, my extremest means,
Lie all unlock'd to your occasions.
Bas. In my school-days, when I had lost one shaft
I shot his fellow of the self-same flight
The self-same way, with more advised watch
To find the other forth; and by adventuring both
I oft found both. I urge this childhood proof,
Because what follows is pure innocence.
I owe you much; and, like a wasteful youth,
That which I owe is lost: but if you please
To shoot another arrow that self way
Which you did shoot the first, I do not doubt,
As I will watch the aim, or to find both,
Or bring your latter hazard back again,
And thankfully rest debtor for the first.
Ant. You know me well; and herein spend but time,
To wind about my love with circumstance;
Then do but say to me what I should do,
That in your knowledge may by me be done,
And I am prest unto it: therefore speak.
Bas. In Belmont is a lady richly left,
And she is fair, and, fairer than that word,
Of wond'rous virtues. Sometimes from her eyes
I did receive fair speechless messages:
Her name is Portia; nothing undervalued
To Cato's daughter, Brutus' Portia.
Nor is the wide world ignorant of her worth;

For the four winds blow in from every coast

Renowned suitors.

O, my Antonio! had I but the means

To hold a rival place with one of them,

I have a mind presages me such thrift.

That I should questionless be fortunate.

Ant. Thou know'st that all my fortunes are at sea;

Neither have I money, nor commodity

To raise a present sum: therefore go forth,

Try what my credit can in Venice do;

That shall be rack'd, even to the uttermost,

To furnish thee to Belmont, to fair Portia.

Go, presently inquire, and so will I,

Where money is; and I no question make,

To have it of my trust, or for my sake.

Exeunt.

SCENE II.—BELMONT. A ROOM IN PORTIA'S HOUSE.

Enter PORTIA and NERISSA.

Por. By my troth, Nerissa, my little body is a-weary of this great world.

Ner. You would be, sweet madam, if your miseries were in the same abundance as your good fortunes are. And yet, for aught I see, they are as sick that surfeit with too much, as they that starve with nothing. It is no small happiness, therefore, to be seated in the mean; superfluity comes sooner by white hairs, but competency lives longer.

Por. Good sentences, and well pronounced.

Ner. They would be better, if well followed.

Por. If to do were as easy as to know what were good to do, chapels had been churches, and poor men's cottages princes' palaces. It is a good divine that follows his own instructions: I can easier teach twenty what were good to be done, than be one of the twenty to follow mine own teaching. But this reasoning is not in the fashion to choose me a husband:—O me, the word choose! I may neither choose whom I would, nor refuse whom I dislike, so is the will of a living daughter curb'd by the will of a dead father:—Is it not hard, Nerissa, that I cannot choose one, nor refuse none?

Ner. Your father was ever virtuous; and holy men at their death have good inspirations; therefore, the lottery that he hath devised in these three chests, of gold, silver, and lead (whereof who chooses his meaning chooses you), will, no doubt, never be chosen by any rightly, but one who you shall rightly love. But what warmth is there in your affection towards any of these princely suitors that are already come?

Por. I pray thee, over-name them; and as thou namest them I will describe them; and according to my description level at my affection.

Ner. First, there is the Neapolitan prince.

Por. Ay, that's a colt, indeed, for he doth nothing but talk of his horse, and he makes it a great approbation of his own good parts that he can shoe him himself.

Ner. Then, is there the county Palatine.

Por. He doth nothing but frown; as who should say, 'An you will not have me, choose;' he hears merry tales, and smiles not: I fear he will prove the weeping philosopher when he grows old, being so full of unmannerly sadness in his youth. I had rather to be married to a death's head with a bone in his mouth, than to either of these. Heaven defend me from these two!

Ner. How say you by the French lord, Monsieur Le Bon?

Por. Heaven made him, and therefore let him pass for a man.

Ner. How like you the young German, the Duke of Saxony's nephew?

Por. Very vilely in the morning, when he is sober; and most vilely in the afternoon, when he is drunk: when he is best he is a little worse than a man; and when he is worst he is little better than a beast: an the worst fall that ever fell, I hope I shall make shift to go without him.

Ner. If he should offer to choose, and choose the right casket, you should refuse to perform your father's will if you should refuse to accept him.

Por. Therefore, for fear of the worst, I pray thee set a deep glass of Rhenish wine on the contrary casket; for, if the devil be within, and that temptation without, I know he will choose it.

Ner. You need not fear, lady, the having any of these lords; they have acquainted me with their determinations: which is, indeed, to return to their home and to trouble you with no more suit; unless you may be won by some other sort than your father's imposition, depending on the caskets.

Por. I am glad this parcel of wooers are so reasonable; for there is not one among them but I dote on his very absence, and I wish them a fair departure.

Ner. Do you not remember, lady, in your father's time, a Venetian, a scholar, and a soldier, that came hither in company of the Marquis of Montferrat?

Por. Yes, yes, it was Bassanio; as I think so was he called.

Ner. True, madam; he, of all the men that ever my foolish eyes looked upon was the best deserving a fair lady.

Por. I remember him well; and I remember him worthy of thy praise.—How now?—What news?

Enter BALTHAZAR.

Ser. The four strangers seek you, madam, to take their leave: and there is a fore-runner come from a fifth, the prince of Morocco; who brings word the prince, his master, will be here to-night.

Por. If I could bid the fifth welcome with so good heart as I can bid the other four farewell, I should be glad of his approach.

Come, Nerissa. Sirrah, go before.

Whiles we shut the gate upon one wooer, another knocks at the door.

Exeunt.

SCENE III.—THE MERCHANT'S EXCHANGE ON THE RIALTO ISLAND. SAN JACOPO, THE MOST ANCIENT CHURCH IN VENICE, OCCUPIES ONE SIDE OF THE SQUARE.

Enter BASSANIO and SHYLOCK.

Shy. Three thousand ducats,—well,

Bas. Ay, sir, for three months.

Shy. For three months,—well.

Bas. For the which, as I told you, Antonio shall be bound.

Shy. Antonio shall become bound,—well.

Bas. May you stead me? Will you pleasure me? Shall I know your answer?

Shy. Three thousand ducats, for three months, and Antonio bound.

Bas. Your answer to that.

Shy. Antonio is a good man.

Bas. Have you heard any imputation to the contrary?

Shy. Oh no, no, no, no;—my meaning in saying he is a good man is, to have you understand me that he is sufficient; yet his means are in supposition: he hath an argosy bound to Tripolis, another to the Indies; I understand, moreover, upon the Rialto, he hath a third at Mexico, a fourth for England; and other ventures he hath, squander'd abroad. But ships are but boards, sailors but men: there be land rats and water rats, land thieves and water thieves; I mean, pirates; and then, there is the peril of waters, winds, and rocks: The man is, notwithstanding, sufficient;—three thousand ducats;—I think I may take his bond.

Bas. Be assured you may.

Shy. I will be assured I may; and that I may be assured I will bethink me: May I speak with Antonio?

Bas. If it please you to dine with us.

Shy. Yes, to smell pork; to eat of the habitation which your prophet, the Nazarite, conjured the devil into! I will buy with you, sell with you, talk with you, walk with you, and so following; but I will not eat with you, drink with you, nor pray with you.—What news on the Rialto?—Who is he comes here?

Bas. This is signior Antonio.

Exit BASSANIO.

Shy. (aside.) How like a fawning publican he looks!

I hate him, for he is a Christian:

But more, for that, in low simplicity,

He lends out money gratis, and brings down

The rate of usance here with us in Venice.

If I can catch him once upon the hip,

I will feed fat the ancient grudge I bear him.
He hates our sacred nation: and he rails
Even there where merchants most do congregate,
On me, my bargains, and my well-won thrift.
Which he calls interest: Cursed be my tribe
If I forgive him!

Re-enter BASSANIO with ANTONIO.

Bas. Shylock, do you hear?
Shy. I am debating of my present store;
And, by the near guess of my memory,
I cannot instantly raise up the gross
Of full three thousand ducats: What of that?
Tubal, a wealthy Hebrew of my tribe,
Will furnish me: But soft: How many months
Do you desire?—Rest you fair, good signior:
To ANTONIO.
Your worship was the last man in our mouths.
Ant. Shylock, albeit, I neither lend nor borrow,
By taking, nor by giving of excess.
Yet, to supply the ripe wants of my friend,
I'll break a custom:—Is he yet possess'd
How much you would?
Shy. Ay, ay, three thousand ducats.
Ant. And for three months.
Shy. I had forgot,—three months, you told me so.
Well then, your bond; and, let me see. But hear you:
Methought you said, you neither lend nor borrow,

Upon advantage.

Ant. I do never use it.

Shy. When Jacob graz'd his uncle Laban's sheep,

This Jacob from our holy Abraham was

(As his wise mother wrought in his behalf)

The third possessor; ay, he was the third.

Ant. And what of him? did he take interest?

Shy. No, not take interest; not, as you would say,

Directly interest: mark what Jacob did.

When Laban and himself were compromis'd

That all the eanlings which were streak'd and pied

Should fall, as Jacob's hire;

The skilful shepherd peel'd me certain wands,

And, in the doing of the deed of kind,

He stuck them up before the fulsome ewes;

Who, then conceiving, did in eaning-time

Fall party-coloured lambs, and those were Jacob's.

This was a way to thrive, and he was blest;

And thrift is blessing, if men steal it not.

Ant. This was a venture, Sir, that Jacob serv'd for;

A thing not in his power to bring to pass,

But sway'd and fashion'd by the hand of Heaven.

Was this inserted to make interest good?

Or is your gold and silver ewes and rams?

Shy. I cannot tell; I make it breed as fast.

Ant. Mark you this, Bassanio,

The devil can cite scripture for his purpose.

An evil soul producing holy witness
Is like a villain with a smiling cheek;
A goodly apple rotten at the heart;
O, what a goodly outside falsehood hath!
Shy. Three thousand ducats,—'tis a good round sum.
Three months from twelve, then let me see the rate.
Ant. Well, Shylock, shall we be beholden to you?
Shy. Signior Antonio, many a time and oft
In the Rialto you have rated me
About my monies, and my usances:
Still have I borne it with a patient shrug;
For sufferance is the badge of all our tribe:
You call me misbeliever, cut-throat dog,
And spet upon my Jewish gaberdine,
And all for use of that which is mine own.
Well, then, it now appears you need my help:
Go to, then; you come to me, and you say,
'Shylock, we would have monies;' You say so;
You, that did void your rheum upon my beard,
And foot me, as you spurn a stranger cur
Over your threshhold; monies is your suit,
What should I say to you? Should I not say
'Hath a dog money? is it possible
A cur can lend three thousand ducats?' or
Shall I bend low, and in a bondman's key,
With 'bated breath, and whispering humbleness,
Say this,—

'Fair Sir, you spet on me on Wednesday last;
You spurn'd me such a day; another time
You call'd me dog; and for these courtesies
I'll lend you thus much monies?'
Ant. I am as like to call thee so again,
To spet on thee again, to spurn thee too.
If thou wilt lend this money, lend it not
As to thy friends; (for when did friendship take
A breed of barren metal of his friend?)
But lend it rather to thine enemy;
Who, if he break, thou may'st with better face
Exact the penalties.
Shy. Why, look you, how you storm!
I would be friends with you, and have your love;
Forget the shames that you have stain'd me with;
Supply your present wants, and take no doit
Of usance for my monies, and you'll not hear me:
This is kind I offer.
Ant. This were kindness.
Shy. This kindness will I show:
Go with me to a notary: seal me there
Your single bond; and, in a merry sport,
If you repay me not on such a day,
In such a place, such sum, or sums, as are
Express'd in the condition, let the forfeit
Be nominated for an equal pound
Of your fair flesh, to be cut off and taken

In what part of your body pleaseth me.
Ant. Content, in faith; I'll seal to such a bond,
And say, there is much kindness in the Jew.
Bas. You shall not seal to such a bond for me
I'll rather dwell in my necessity.
Ant. Why, fear not, man; I will not forfeit it;
Within these two months, that's a month before
This bond expires, I do expect return
Of thrice three times the value of this bond.
Shy. O father Abraham, what these Christians are.
Whose own hard dealings teaches them suspect
The thoughts of others! Pray you, tell me this
If he should break his day, what should I gain
By the exaction of the forfeiture?
A pound of man's flesh, taken from a man,
Is not so estimable, profitable neither,
As flesh of muttons, beefs, or goats. I say,
To buy his favour I extend this friendship;
If he will take it, so; if not, adieu;
And, for my love, I pray you wrong me not.
Ant. Yes, Shylock, I will seal unto this bond.
Shy. Then meet me forthwith at the notary's;
Give him direction for this merry bond,
And I will go and purse the ducats straight;
See to my house, left in the fearful guard
Of an unthrifty knave; and presently
I will be with you.

Exit.

Ant. Hie thee, gentle Jew.

This Hebrew will turn Christian; he grows kind.

Bas. I like not fair terms and a villain's mind.

Ant. Come, on; in this there can be no dismay,

My ships come home a month before the day.

Exeunt.

SCENE IV.—SALOON OF THE CASKETS IN PORTIA'S HOUSE, AT BELMONT.

Flourish of Cornets. Enter the PRINCE OF MOROCCO, and his Train; PORTIA, NERISSA, and other of her Attendants.

Mor. Mislike me not for my complexion,

The shadow'd livery of the burning sun,

To whom I am a neighbour, and near bred.

Bring me the fairest creature northward born,

Where Phoebus' fire scarce thaws the icicles,

And let us make incision for your love,

To prove whose blood is reddest, his or mine.

By love, I swear, I would not change this hue,

Except to steal your thoughts, my gentle queen.

I'll try my fortune;

E'en though I may (blind fortune leading me)

Miss that which one unworthier may attain,

And die with grieving.

Por. You must take your chance;

And either not attempt to choose at all,

Or swear, before you choose,—if you choose wrong,

Never to speak to lady afterward
In way of marriage; therefore be advis'd.
Mor. Nor will not; come, bring me unto my chance.
How shall I know if I do choose the right?
Por. The one of them contains my picture, prince;
If you choose that, then I am yours withal.
Mor. Some god direct my judgment! Let me see.
The first, of gold, who this inscription bears:
"Who chooseth me shall gain what many men desire."
The second, silver, which this promise carries:
"Who chooseth me shall get as much as he deserves."
The third, dull lead, with warning all as blunt:
"Who chooseth me must give and hazard all he hath."
One of these three contains her heavenly picture.
Is't like that lead contains her? 'Twere perdition
To think so base a thought;
Or shall I think in silver she's immur'd,
Being ten times undervalued to tried gold?
O sinful thought. Never so rich a gem
Was set in worse than gold.
Deliver me the key;
Here do I choose, and thrive I as I may!
Por. There, take it prince, and if my form lie there,
Then I am yours.
He unlocks the golden casket.
Mor. What have we here?
A carrion death, within whose empty eye

There is a written scroll. I'll read the writing.

"All that glitters is not gold,Often have you heard that told:

"Had you been as wise as bold,Young in limbs, in judgment old,Your answer had not been inscrol'd:Fare you well; your suit is cold."

Cold, indeed; and labour lost:

Then, farewell, heat; and welcome frost—Portia,

adieu! I have too griev'd a heart

To take a tedious leave: thus losers part.

Exit.

Por. A gentle riddance:—go:—

Let all of his complexion choose me so.

END OF ACT FIRST.

ACT II.

SCENE I.—VENICE. EXTERIOR OF SHYLOCK'S HOUSE.

Enter LAUNCELOT GOBBO.

Lau. Certainly my conscience will serve me to run from this Jew, my master: The fiend is at mine elbow, and tempts me; saying to me,—Gobbo, Launcelot Gobbo, good Launcelot, or good Gobbo, or good Launcelot Gobbo, use your legs, take the start, run away:—My conscience says,—No: take heed, honest Launcelot; take heed, honest Gobbo: or (as aforesaid) honest Launcelot Gobbo; do not run: scorn running with thy heels. Well the most courageous fiend bids me pack. Via! says the fiend; Away! says the fiend, for the heavens; rouse up a brave mind, says the fiend, and run. Well, my conscience, hanging about the neck of my heart, says very wisely to me, my honest friend, Launcelot, being an honest man's son, or rather an honest woman's son;—for, indeed, my father did something smack, something grow to, he had a kind of taste;—well, my conscience says, Launcelot, budge not; budge, says the fiend; budge not, says my conscience. Conscience, say I, you counsel well; fiend, say I, you counsel well; to be ruled by my conscience I should stay with the Jew, my master, who (Heaven bless the mark!) is a kind of devil; and to run away from the Jew I should be ruled by the fiend, who, saving your reverence, is the devil himself. Certainly, the Jew is the very devil incarnation; and in my conscience, my conscience is a kind of hard conscience, to offer to counsel me to stay with the Jew. The fiend gives the more friendly counsel: I will run, fiend; my heels are at your commandment, I will run.

As he is going out in haste

Enter OLD GOBBO, with a basket.

Gob. Master, young man, you, I pray you; which is the way to master Jew's?

Lau. (aside.) O heavens, this is my true-begotten father! who, being more than sand-blind, high-gravel blind, knows me not: I will try conclusions with him.

Gob. Master young gentleman, I pray you which is the way to master Jew's?

Lau. Turn upon your right hand at the next turning, but, at the next turning of all, on your left; marry, at the very next turning, turn of no hand, but turn down indirectly to the Jew's house.

Gob. 'Twill be a hard way to hit. Can you tell me whether one Launcelot that dwells with him, dwell with him, or no?

Lau, Talk you of young master Launcelot?—mark me, now—(aside.)—now will I raise the waters. Talk you of young master Launcelot?

Gob. No master, sir: but a poor man's son: his father, though I say it, is an honest exceeding poor man, and, Heaven be thanked, well to live.

Lau, Well, let his father be what he will, we talk of young master Launcelot.

Gob. Of Launcelot, an't please your mastership.

Lau. Ergo, master Launcelot; talk not of master Launcelot, father; for the young gentleman (according to fates and destinies, and such odd sayings, the sisters three, and such branches of learning), is, indeed, deceased; or, as you would say in plain terms, gone to heaven.

Gob. Marry, Heaven forbid! the boy was the very staff of my age, my very prop.

Lau. Do I look like a cudgel, or a hovel-post, a staff, or a prop?—Do you know me, father?

Gob. Alack the day, I know you not, young gentleman; but, I pray you tell me, is my boy (rest his soul!) alive or dead?

Lau. Do you not know me, father?

Gob. Alack! sir, I am sand-blind, I know you not.

Lau. Nay, indeed, if you had your eyes, you might fail of the knowing me: it is a wise father that knows his own child. Well, old man, I will tell you news of your son: Give me your blessing: (kneels.) Truth will come to light; murder cannot be hid long; a man's son may; but, in the end, truth will out.

Gob. Pray you, sir, stand up: I am sure you are not Launcelot, my boy.

Lau. Pray you, let's have no more fooling about it, but give me your blessing; I am Launcelot, your boy that was, your son that is, your child that shall be.

Gob. I cannot think you are my son.

Lau. I know not what I shall think of that; but I am Launcelot, the Jew's man; and I am sure Margery, your wife, is my mother.

Gob. Her name is Margery, indeed: I'll be sworn if thou be Launcelot, thou art mine own flesh and blood. What a beard hast thou got: thou hast got more hair on thy chin than Dobbin, my phill-horse, has on his tail.

Lau. It should seem, then, that Dobbin's tail grows backward; I am sure he had more hair of his tail than I have of my face, when I last saw him.

Gob. Lord, how art thou changed! How dost thou and thy master agree? I have brought him a present.

Lau. (rises.) Give him a present! give him a halter: I am famished in his service; you may tell every finger I have with my ribs. Father, I am glad you are come: give me your present to one master Bassanio, who, indeed, gives rare new liveries; if I serve not him, I will run as far as Heaven has any ground.—O rare fortune! here comes the man;—to him, father; for I am a Jew if I serve the Jew any longer.

Enter BASSANIO, with LEONARDO, and STEPHANO.

Bas. See these letters deliver'd; put the liveries to making; and desire Gratiano to come anon to my lodging.

Exit a SERVANT.

Lau. To him, father.

Gob. Heaven bless your worship!

Bas. Gramercy! Would'st thou aught with me?

Gob. Here's my son, sir, a poor boy—

Lau. Not a poor boy, sir; but the rich Jew's man; that would, sir, as my father shall specify.

Gob. He hath a great infection, sir, as one would say, to serve——

Lau. Indeed, the short and the long is, I serve the Jew, and have a desire as my father shall specify.

Gob. His master and he (saving your worship's reverence) are scarce cater-cousins.

Lau. To be brief, the very truth is, that the Jew having done me wrong, doth cause me, as my father, being I hope an old man, shall frutify unto you.

Gob. I have here a dish of doves, that I would bestow upon your worship; and my suit is——

Lau. In very brief, the suit is impertinent to myself, as your worship shall know by this honest old man; and, though I say it, though old man, yet poor man, my father.

Bas. One speak for both. What would you?

Lau. Serve you, sir.

Gob. That is the very defect of the matter, sir.

Bas. I know thee well; thou hast obtain'd thy suit:

Shylock, thy master, spoke with me this day,

And hath preferr'd thee, if it be preferment,

To leave a rich Jew's service, to become

The follower of so poor a gentleman.

Lau. The old proverb is very well parted between my master, Shylock, and you, sir; you have the grace of Heaven, sir, and he hath—— enough.

Bas. Thou speak'st it well. Go, father, with thy son:—

Take leave of thy old master, and inquire

My lodging out:—give him a livery. To his Followers.

More guarded than his fellows': See it done.

Lau. Father, in:—(Exit OLD GOBBO.) I cannot get a service, no!—I have ne'er a tongue in my head!—Well; (looking on his palm) if any man in Italy have a fairer table;which doth offer to swear upon a book I shall have good fortune! Go to, here's a simple line of life! here's a small trifle of wives: Alas, fifteen wives is nothing; eleven widows and nine maids, is a simple coming in for one man: and then, to 'scape drowning thrice; and to be in peril of my life with the edge of a feather-bed, here are simple 'scapes! Well, if fortune be a woman she's a good wench for this gear.—I'll take my leave of the Jew in the twinkling of an eye.

Exit LAUNCELOT.

Bas. I pray thee, good Leonardo, think on this; These things being bought and orderly bestow'd, Return in haste, for I do feast to-night My best-esteem'd acquaintance: hie thee, go.

Leo. My best endeavours shall be done herein.

Enter GRATIANO.

Gra. Where is your master?

Leo. Yonder, sir, he walks.

Exit LEONARDO

Gra. Signior Bassanio,—

Bas. Gratiano!

Gra. I have a suit to you.

Bas. You have obtained it.

Gra. You must not deny me: I must go with you to Belmont.

Bas. Why, then you must.—But hear thee, Gratiano;

Thou art too wild, too rude, and bold of voice;

Parts, that become thee happily enough,

And in such eyes as ours appear not faults;

But, where they are not known, why, there they show

Something too liberal:—pray thee take pain

To allay with some cold drops of modesty

Thy skipping spirit; lest, through thy wild behaviour,

I be misconstrued in the place I go to,

And lose my hopes.

Gra. Signior Bassanio, hear me:

If I do not put on a sober habit,

Talk with respect, and swear but now and then,

Wear prayer-books in my pocket, look demurely;

Nay more, while grace is saying, hood mine eyes

Thus with my hat, and sigh, and say amen;

Use all the observance of civility,

Like one well studied in a sad ostent;

To please his grandam,—never trust me more.

Bas, Well, we shall see your bearing.

Gra. Nay, but I bar to-night; you shall not gage me

By what we do to-night.

Bas. No, that were pity;

I would entreat you rather to put on

Your boldest suit of mirth, for we have friends

That purpose merriment: But fare you well,

I have some business.

Gra. And I must to Lorenzo and the rest;

But we will visit you at supper time.

Exeunt.
Enter JESSICA and LAUNCELOT from SHYLOCK'S house.

Jes. I am sorry thou wilt leave my father so;

Our house is hell, and thou, a merry devil,

Didst rob it of some taste of tediousness:

But fare thee well: there is a ducat for thee;

And, Launcelot, soon at supper shall thou see

Lorenzo, who is thy new master's guest:

Give him this letter; do it secretly,

And so farewell; I would not have my father

See me in talk with thee.

Lau. Adieu!—Tears exhibit my tongue. Most beautiful pagan,—most sweet Jew! Adieu! these foolish drops do somewhat drown my manly spirit: adieu.

Exit.

Jes. Farewell, good Launcelot.

Alack, what heinous sin is it in me,

To be asham'd to be my father's child!

But though I am a daughter to his blood,

I am not to his manners: O Lorenzo,

If thou keep promise, I shall end this strife;

Become a Christian, and thy loving wife.

Exit into house.

Enter GRATIANO, LORENZO, SALARINO, and SALANIO.

Lor. Nay, we will slink away in supper time;

Disguise us at my lodging, and return

All in an hour.

Gra. We have not made good preparation.

Salar. We have not spoke us yet of torch-bearers.

Sal. 'Tis vile, unless it may be quaintly order'd;

And better, in my mind, not undertook.

Lor. 'Tis now but four o'clock; we have two hours

To furnish us.—

Enter LAUNCELOT with a letter.

Friend Launcelot, what's the news?

Lau. An it shall please you to break up this, it shall seem to signify.

Lor. I know the hand: in faith, 'tis a fair hand;

And whiter than the paper it writ on

Is the fair hand that writ.

Gra. Love-news, in faith.

Lau. By your leave, sir.

Lor. Whither goest thou?

Lau. Marry, sir, to bid my old master the Jew to sup to-night with my new master the Christian.

Lor. Hold here, take this:—tell gentle Jessica, I will not fail her;—speak it privately; go.

Exit LAUNCELOT into house.

Gentlemen,

Will you prepare you for this masque to-night?

I am provided of a torch-bearer.

Salar. Ay, marry, I'll be gone about it straight.

Sal. And so will I.

Lor. Meet me and Gratiano

At Gratiano's lodging some hour hence.

Salar. 'Tis good we do so.

Exeunt SALARINO and SALANIO.

Gra. Was not that letter from fair Jessica?

Lor. I must needs tell thee all: She hath directed

How I shall take her from her father's house;

What gold and jewels she is furnish'd with;

Come, go with me; peruse this as thou goest:

Fair Jessica shall be my torch-bearer.

Exeunt.
Enter SHYLOCK and LAUNCELOT from House.

Shy. Well, thou shalt see, thy eyes shall be thy judge,

The difference of old Shylock and Bassanio:

What, Jessica!—thou shalt not gormandize,

As thou hast done with me;—What, Jessica!—

And sleep and snore, and rend apparel out;—

Why, Jessica, I say!

Lau. Why, Jessica!

Shy. Who bids thee call? I do not bid thee call.

Lau. Your worship was wont to tell me I could do nothing without bidding.

Enter JESSICA.

Jes. Call you? What is your will?

Shy. I am bid forth to supper, Jessica;

There are my keys:—But wherefore should I go?

I am not bid for love: they flatter me:

But yet I'll go in hate, to feed upon

The prodigal Christian:—Jessica, my girl,

Look to my house:—I am right loath to go;

There is some ill a brewing towards my rest,

For I did dream of money-bags to night.

Lau. I beseech you, sir, go; my young master doth expect your reproach.

Shy. So do I his.

Lau. And they have conspired together,—I will not say, you shall see a masque; but if you do, then it was not for nothing that my nose fell a bleeding on Black Monday last, at six o'clock i'the morning, falling out that year on Ash-Wednesday was four year in the afternoon.

Shy. What! are there masques? Hear you me, Jessica:

Lock up my doors; and when you hear the drum,

And the vile squeaking of the wry-neck'd fife,

Clamber not you up to the casements then,

Nor thrust your head into the public street,

To gaze on Christian fools with varnish'd faces:

But stop my house's ears, I mean my casements;

Let not the sound of shallow foppery enter

My sober house.—By Jacob's staff I swear,

I have no mind of feasting forth to-night:

But I will go.—Go you before me, sirrah;

Say, I will come.

Lau. I will go before, Sir.—

Mistress, look out at window, for all this;

There will come a Christian by,

Will be worth a Jewess' eye.

Exit LAUNCELOT.

Shy. What says that fool of Hagar's offspring, ha?

Jes. His words were, Farewell, mistress; nothing else.

Shy. The patch is kind enough; but a huge feeder,

Snail-slow in profit, and he sleeps by day

More than the wild cat: drones hive not with me,

Therefore I part with him; and part with him

To one that I would have him help to waste

His borrow'd purse.—Well, Jessica, go in;

Perhaps, I will return immediately;

Do as I bid you,

Shut doors after you: Fast bind, fast find;

A proverb never stale in thrifty mind.

Exit.

Jes. Farewell; and if my fortune be not crost,

I have a father, you a daughter, lost.

Exit into house.
Enter GRATIANO and SALARINO, masqued.

Gra. This is the pent-house, under which Lorenzo

Desir'd us to make stand.

Sal. His hour is almost past.

Gra. And it is marvel he out-dwells his hour,

For lovers ever run before the clock.

Sal. O, ten times faster Venus' pigeons fly

To seal love's bonds new made, than they are wont

To keep obliged faith unforfeited!

Gra. That ever holds: who riseth from a feast,

With that keen appetite that he sits down?

Where is the horse that doth untread again

His tedious measures with the unbated fire

That he did pace them first? All things that are,

Are with more spirit chased than enjoy'd.

Enter LORENZO.

Sal. Here comes Lorenzo.

Lor. Sweet friends, your patience for my long abode:

Not I, but my affairs, have made you wait:

When you shall please to play the thieves for wives,

I'll watch as long for you then.—

Here dwells my father Jew:—

GLEE.

O happy fair!Your eyes are lode-stars, and your tongue sweet air!More tuneable than lark to shepherd's earWhen wheat is green, when hawthorn buds appear!

Ho! who's within?

Enter JESSICA, above.

Jes. Who are you? Tell me, for more certainty,

Albeit I'll swear that I do know your tongue.

Lor. Lorenzo, and thy love.

Jes. Lorenzo, certain; and my love, indeed;

For who love I so much? And now who knows

But you, Lorenzo, whether I am yours?

Lor. Heaven, and thy thoughts, are witness that thou art.

Jes. Here, catch this casket; it is worth the pains.

Lor. Come, come at once;

For the close night doth play the run-away,

And we are staid for at Bassanio's feast.

Jes. I will make fast the doors, and gild myself

With some more ducats, and be with you straight.

Exit from above.

Gra. Now, by my hood, a Gentile and no Jew.

Lor. Beshrew me, but I love her heartily:

For she is wise, if I can judge of her;

And fair she is, if that mine eyes be true;

And true she is, as she hath prov'd herself;

And therefore, like herself, wise, fair, and true,

Shall she be placed in my constant soul.

Enter JESSICA, below.

What, art thou come?—On, gentlemen, away;

Our masquing mates by this time for us stay.

Exeunt

Enter various parties of Maskers, Revellers, &c.

END OF SECOND ACT.

ACT III.

SCENE I.—SALOON OF THE CASKETS IN PORTIA'S HOUSE AT BELMONT.

Enter NERISSA, with SERVANTS.

Ner. The prince of Arragon hath ta'en his oath,

And comes to his election presently.

Flourish of Trumpets.

Enter the PRINCE OF ARRAGON, PORTIA, and their Trains.

Por. Behold, there stand the caskets, noble prince;

If you choose that wherein I am contain'd,

Straight shall our nuptial rites be solemniz'd;

But if you fail, without more speech, my lord,

You must be gone from hence immediately.

Arr. I am enjoin'd by oath to observe three things:

First, never to unfold to any one

Which casket 'twas I chose; next, if I fail

Of the right casket, never in my life

To woo a maid in way of marriage; lastly,

If I do fail in fortune of my choice,

Immediately to leave you and be gone.

Por. To these injunctions every one doth swear

That comes to hazard for my worthless self.

Arr. And so have I address'd me: Fortune now

To my heart's hope!—Gold, silver, and base lead.

'Who chooseth me must give and hazard all he hath.'

What says the golden chest? ha! let me see:

'Who chooseth me shall gain what many men desire.'

What many men desire.—That many may be meant

By the fool multitude, that choose by show,

Why, then, to thee, thou silver treasure-house;

Tell me once more what title thou dost bear:

'Who chooseth me shall get as much as he deserves;'

And well said too. For who shall go about

To cozen fortune, and be honourable

Without the stamp of merit!

O, that estates, degrees, and offices,

Were not deriv'd corruptly! and that clear honour

Were purchas'd by the merit of the wearer!

How many then should cover that stand bare?

How many be commanded that command?

And how much honour

Pick'd from the chaff and ruin of the times,

To be new varnish'd? Well, but to my choice:

'Who chooseth me shall get as much as he deserves:'

I will assume desert:—Give me a key for this,

And instantly unlock my fortunes here.

Por. Too long a pause for that which you find there.

Arr. What's here: the portrait of a blinking idiot,

Presenting me a schedule? I will read it.

Some there be that shadows kiss;Such have but a shadow's bliss:There be fools alive, I wis,Silver'd o'er; and so was this.'

Still more fool I shall appearBy the time I linger here:With one fool's head I came to woo,But I go away with two.

Sweet, adieu! I'll keep my oath,

Patiently to bear my wroath.

Exeunt ARRAGON and Train.

Por. Thus hath the candle sing'd the moth.

O these deliberate fools! when they do choose,

They have the wisdom by their wit to lose.

Ner. The ancient saying is no heresy;—

Hanging and wiving goes by destiny.

Enter BALTHAZAR.

Ser. Madam, there is alighted at your gate

A young Venetian, one that comes before

To signify the approaching of his lord:

From whom he bringeth sensible regreets;

To wit, besides commends and courteous breath,

Gifts of rich value; yet I have not seen

So likely an ambassador of love.

Por. No more, I pray thee.

Come, come, Nerissa; for I long to see

Quick Cupid's post that comes so mannerly.

Ner. Bassanio, lord love, if thy will it be!

Exeunt.

SCENE II.—RIALTO BRIDGE , AND GRAND CANAL.

Enter SALARINO and SALANIO.

Salar. Why, man, I saw Bassanio under sail;

With him is Gratiano gone along;

And in their ship, I am sure, Lorenzo is not.

Sal. The villain Jew with outcries rais'd the duke;

Who went with him to search Bassanio's ship.

Salar. He came too late, the ship was under sail;

But there the duke was given to understand,

That in a gondola were seen together

Lorenzo and his amorous Jessica;

Besides, Antonio certified the duke,

They were not with Bassanio in his ship.

Sal. I never heard a passion so confus'd,

So strange, outrageous, and so variable,

As the dog Jew did utter in the streets;

"My daughter!—O, my ducats!—O, my daughter!

Fled with a Christian!—O, my Christian ducats!—

Justice! the law! my ducats, and my daughter.!"

Let good Antonio look he keep his day,

Or he shall pay for this.

Salar. Marry, well remember'd: I reason'd with a Frenchman yesterday, who told me that Antonio hath a ship of rich lading wreck'd on the narrow seas that part the French and English,—the Goodwins, I think they call the place—a very dangerous flat and fatal, where the carcases of many a tall ship lie buried, as they say, if my gossip report be an honest woman of her word.

Sal. I would she were as lying a gossip in that, as ever knapp'd ginger, or made her neighbours believe she wept for the death of a third husband: But it is true, that the good Antonio, the honest Antonio,—O, that I had a title good enough to keep his name company!—

Salar. Come, the full stop.

Sal. Why, the end is, he hath lost a ship.

Salar. I would it might prove the end of his losses!

Sal. Let me say amen betimes, lest the devil cross my prayer; for here he comes in the likeness of a Jew.

Enter SHYLOCK.

Salar. How now, Shylock? what news among the merchants?

Shy. You knew, none so well, none so well as you, of my daughter's flight?

Sal. That's certain. I, for my part, knew the tailor that made the wings she flew withal.

Salar. And Shylock, for his own part, knew the bird was fledg'd; and then it is the complexion of them all to leave the dam.

Shy. She is damn'd for it.

Sal. That's certain, if the devil may be her judge.

Shy. My own flesh and blood to rebel!

Salar. But tell us, do you hear whether Antonio have had any loss at sea or no?

Shy. There I have another bad match: a bankrupt, a prodigal, who dare scarce show his head on the Rialto; a beggar, that used to come so smug upon the mart.—Let him look to his bond: he was wont to call me usurer;—let him look to his bond: he was wont to lend money for a Christian courtesy;—let him look to his bond.

Sal. Why, I am sure, if he forfeit, thou wilt not take his flesh? What's that good for?

Shy. To bait fish withal: if it will feed nothing else it will feed my revenge. He hath disgraced me, and hindered me half a million; laughed at my losses, mocked at my gains, scorned my nation, thwarted my bargains, cooled my friends, heated mine enemies: and what's his reason? I am a Jew. Hath not a Jew eyes? hath not a Jew hands, organs, dimensions, senses, affections, passions? fed with the same food, hurt with the same weapons, subject to the same diseases, healed by the same means, warmed and cooled by the same winter and summer as a Christian is? If you prick us, do we not bleed? if you tickle us, do we not laugh? if you poison us, do we not die? and if you wrong us, shall we not revenge? If we are like you in the rest, we will resemble you in that. If a Jew wrong a Christian, what is his humility? revenge: If a Christian wrong a Jew, what should his sufferance be by Christian example? why, revenge. The villany you teach me I will execute: and it shall go hard but I will better the instruction.

Salar. Here comes another of the tribe; a third cannot be matched, unless the devil himself turn Jew.

Exeunt SALANIO, SALARINO, and Servant.

Enter TUBAL.

Shy. How now, Tubal, what news from Genoa? hast thou found my daughter?

Tub. I often came where I did hear of her, but cannot find her.

Shy. Why, there, there, there, there! a diamond gone, cost me two thousand ducats in Frankfort! The curse never fell upon our nation till now; I never felt it till now:—two thousand ducats in that; and other precious, precious jewels. —I would my daughter were dead at my foot, and the jewels in her ear! 'would she were hears'd at my foot, and the ducats in her coffin! No news of them?—Why, so:—and I know not what's spent in the search: Why, thou loss upon loss! the thief gone with so much, and so much to find the thief; and no satisfaction, no revenge: nor no ill luck stirring but what lights o' my shoulders; no sighs but o' my breathing; no tears but o' my shedding.

Tub. Yes, other men have ill luck, too. Antonio, as I heard in Genoa,—

Shy. What, what, what? ill luck, ill luck?

Tub. Hath an argosy cast away, coming from Tripolis.

Shy. I thank God, I thank God:—Is it true? is it true?

Tub. I spoke with some of the sailors that escaped the wreck.

Shy. I thank thee, good Tubal;—Good news, good news: ha! ha!—Where? in Genoa?

Tub. Your daughter spent in Genoa, as I heard, one night, fourscore ducats!

Shy. Thou stick'st a dagger in me:—I shall never see my gold again: Fourscore ducats at a sitting! fourscore ducats!

Tub. There came divers of Antonio's creditors in my company to Venice, that swear he cannot choose but break.

Shy. I am very glad of it: I'll plague him; I'll torture him; I am glad of it.

Tub. One of them showed me a ring, that he had of your daughter for a monkey.

Shy. Out upon her! Thou torturest me, Tubal: it was my turquoise; I had it of Leah, when I was a bachelor: I would not have given it for a wilderness of monkeys.

Tub. But Antonio is certainly undone.

Shy. Nay, that's true, that's very true: Go, Tubal, fee me an officer, bespeak him a fortnight before: I will have the heart of him, if he forfeit; for were he out of Venice, I can make what merchandize I will. Go, Tubal, and meet me at our synagogue: go, good Tubal; at our synagogue, Tubal.

Exeunt.

SCENE III.—SALOON OF THE CASKETS, IN PORTIA'S HOUSE, AT BELMONT.

BASSANIO, PORTIA, GRATIANO, NERISSA, and Attendants.

Por. I pray you, tarry; pause a day or two,

Before you hazard; for, in choosing wrong

I lose your company; I could teach you

How to choose right, but then I am forsworn;

So will I never be: so may you miss me;

But if you do, you'll make me wish a sin,

That I had been forsworn.

Bas. Let me choose;

For, as I am, I live upon the rack.

Come, let me to my fortune and the caskets.

Por. Away then: I am lock'd in one of them;

If you do love me, you will find me out.

Let music sound, while he doth make his choice:

Then, if he lose, he makes a swan-like end,

Fading in music.—That the comparison

May stand more proper, my eye shall be the stream

And wat'ry death-bed for him.

Music, whilst BASSANIO comments on the Caskets to himself.

SONG.

1. Tell me where is fancy bred.Or in the heart, or in the head?How begot, how nourishedReply, reply.

2. It is engender'd in the eyes,With gazing fed; and fancy diesIn the cradle where it lies:Let us all ring fancy's knell;I'll begin it.—Ding, dong, bell.All. Ding, dong, bell.

Exeunt all but PORTIA and BASSANIO.

Bas. So may the outward shows be least themselves;

The world is still deceiv'd with ornament.

In law, what plea so tainted and corrupt,

But, being season'd with a gracious voice,

Obscures the show of evil? In religion,

What damned error, but some sober brow

Will bless it and approve it with a text,

Hiding the grossness with fair ornament?

There is no vice so simple, but assumes

Some mark of virtue on his outward parts.

Thus ornament is but the guiled shore

To a most dangerous sea; the beauteous scarf

Veiling an Indian beauty. Therefore, thou gaudy gold,

Hard food for Midas, I will none of thee:

Nor none of thee, thou pale and common drudge

'Tween man and man. But thou, thou meagre lead,

Which rather threat'nest than dost promise aught,

Thy plainness moves me more than eloquence,

And here choose I. Joy be the consequence!

Por. How all the other passions fleet to air!

O love, be moderate, allay thy ecstacy,

I feel too much thy blessing, make it less,

For fear I surfeit!

Bas. What find I here!

Opening the leaden casket.

Fair Portia's counterfeit?—Here's the scroll,

The continent and summary of my fortune.

'You that choose not by the view,Chance as felt, and choose as true!Since this fortune falls to you,Be content, and seek no new.If you be well pleas'd with this,And hold your fortune for your bliss.Turn you where your lady is,And claim her with a loving kiss.'

A gentle scroll.—Fair lady, by your leave,

I come by note, to give and to receive.

Yet doubtful whether what I see be true,

Until confirm'd, sign'd, ratified by you.

Por. You see, my lord Bassanio, where I stand,

Such as I am: though, for myself alone,

I would not be ambitious in my wish,

To wish myself much better; yet, for you,

I would be trebled twenty times myself.

But now I was the lord

Of this fair mansion, master of my servants,

Queen o'er myself; and even now, but now,

This house, these servants, and this same myself.

Are yours, my lord,—I give them with this ring;

Which, when you part from, lose, or give away,

Let it presage the ruin of your love,

And be my vantage to exclaim on you.

Bas. Madam, you have bereft me of all words;

Only my blood speaks to you in my veins:

But when this ring

Parts from this finger, then parts life from hence;

O, then be bold to say, Bassanio's dead.

Ner. My lord and lady, it is now our time,
That have stood by and seen our wishes prosper,
To cry good joy; God joy, my lord and lady!
Gra. My lord Bassanio, and my gentle lady,
I wish you all the joy that you can wish;
For I am sure you can wish none from me:
And, when your honours mean to solemnize
The bargain of your faith, I do beseech you
Even at that time I may be married too.
Bas. With all my heart, so thou canst get a wife.
Gra. I thank your lordship; you have got me one.
My eyes, my lord, can look as swift as yours:
You saw the mistress, I beheld the maid;
You lov'd, I lov'd; for intermission
No more pertains to me, my lord, than you.
Your fortune stood upon the caskets there;
And so did mine too, as the matter falls:
For wooing here, until my roof was dry
With oaths of love, at last,—if promise last,—
I got a promise of this fair one here,
To have her love, provided that your fortune
Achiev'd her mistress.
Por. Is this true, Nerissa?
Ner. Madam, it is, so you stand pleas'd withal.
Bas. And do you, Gratiano, mean good faith?
Gra. Yes, faith, my lord.
Bas. Our feast shall be much honour'd in your marriage.

Gra. But who comes here? Lorenzo, and his infidel?

What, and my old Venetian friend, Solanio.

Enter LORENZO, JESSICA, and SALANIO.

Bas. Lorenzo, and Solanio, welcome hither;

If that the youth of my new interest here

Have power to bid you welcome:—By your leave,

I bid my very friends and countrymen,

Sweet Portia, welcome.

Por. So do I, my lord;

They are entirely welcome.

Lor. I thank your honour:—For my part, my lord,

My purpose was not to have seen you here;

But meeting with Solanio by the way,

He did entreat me, past all saying nay,

To come with him along.

Sal. I did, my lord,

And I have reason for it. Signior Antonio

Commends him to you.

Gives BASSANIO a letter.

Bas. Ere I ope this letter,

I pray you tell me how my good friend doth.

Sal. Not sick, my lord, unless it be in mind:

Nor well, unless in mind: his letter there

Will show you his estate.

Gra. Nerissa, cheer yon stranger; bid her welcome.

Your hand, Solanio. What's the news from Venice?

How doth that royal merchant, good Antonio?

I know he will be glad of our success;
We are the Jasons, we have won the fleece.
Sal. 'Would you had won the fleece that he hath lost!
Por. There are some shrewd contents in yon same paper,
That steal the colour from Bassanio's cheek;
Some dear friend dead; else nothing in the world
Could turn so much the constitution
Of any constant man. What, worse and worse?—
With leave, Bassanio; I am half yourself,
And I must freely have the half of any thing
That this same paper brings you.
Bas. O sweet Portia,
Here are a few of the unpleasant'st words
That ever blotted paper! Gentle lady,
When I did first impart my love to you,
I freely told you, all the wealth I had
Ran in my veins,—I was a gentleman:
And then I told you true: and yet, dear lady,
Rating myself at nothing, you shall see
How much I was a braggart: When I told you
My state was nothing, I should then have told you
That I was worse than nothing; for, indeed,
I have engag'd myself to a dear friend,
Engag'd my friend to his mere enemy,
To feed my means. Here is a letter, lady;
The paper as the body of my friend,
And every word in it a gaping wound,

Issuing life-blood. But is it true, Solanio?
Have all his ventures fail'd? What, not one hit?
From Tripolis, from Mexico, and England,
From Lisbon, Barbary, and India?
And not one vessel 'scape the dreadful touch
Of merchant-marring rocks?
Sal. Not one, my lord.
Besides, it should appear, that if he had
The present money to discharge the Jew,
He would not take it: Never did I know
A creature that did bear the shape of man,
So keen and greedy to confound a man.
He plies the duke at morning, and at night;
And doth impeach the freedom of the state
If they deny him justice: twenty merchants,
The duke himself, and the magnificoes
Of greatest port, have all persuaded with him;
But none can drive him from the envious plea
Of forfeiture, of justice, and his bond.
Por. Is it your dear friend that is thus in trouble?
Bas. The dearest friend to me, the kindest man,
The best condition'd and unwearied spirit
In doing courtesies, and one in whom
The ancient Roman honour more appears,
Than any that draws breath in Italy.
Por. What sum owes he the Jew?
Bas. For me, three thousand ducats.

Por. What, no more?

Pay him six thousand, and deface the bond;

Double six thousand, and then treble that,

Before a friend of this description

Shall lose a hair through Bassanio's fault.

First, go with me to church, and call me wife:

And then away to Venice to your friend!

For never shall you stay by Portia's side

With an unquiet soul. You shall have gold

To pay the petty debt twenty times over;

When it is paid, bring your true friend along:

My maid Nerissa, and myself, mean time,

Will live as maids and widows. Come, away;

For you shall hence, upon my wedding-day:

But let me hear the letter of your friend.

Bas. (reads.)

'Sweet Bassanio, my ships have all miscarried, my creditors grow cruel, my estate is very low, my bond to the Jew is forfeit; and since, in paying it, it is impossible I should live, all debts are cleared between you and me, if I might but see you at my death: notwithstanding, use your pleasure: if your love do not persuade you to come, let not my letter.'

Por. O love, despatch all business, and be gone.

Bas. Since I have your good leave to go away,

I will make haste: but, till I come again,

No bed shall e'er be guilty of my stay,

Nor rest be interposer 'twixt us twain.

Exeunt.

SCENE IV.—VENICE. THE COLUMNS OF ST. MARK.

Enter SHYLOCK, SALARINO, ANTONIO, and GAOLER.

Shy, Gaoler, look to him. Tell not me of mercy;—

This is the fool that lends out money gratis;—

Gaoler, look to him.

Ant. Hear me yet, good Shylock.

Shy. I'll have my bond; speak not against my bond;

I have sworn an oath that I will have my bond:

Thou call'dst me dog, before thou had'st a cause:

But, since I am a dog, beware my fangs:

The duke shall grant me justice.—I do wonder,

Thou naughty gaoler, that thou art so fond

To come abroad with him at his request.

Ant. I pray thee, hear me speak.

Shy. I'll have my bond; I will not hear thee speak:

I'll have my bond; and therefore speak no more.

I'll not be made a soft and dull-ey'd fool,

To shake the head, relent, and sigh, and yield

To Christian intercessors. Follow not;

I'll have no speaking; I will have my bond.

Exit SHYLOCK.

Salar. It is the most impenetrable cur

That ever kept with men.

Ant. Let him alone;

I'll follow him no more with bootless prayers.

He seeks my life.

Salar. I am sure the duke

Will never grant this forfeiture to hold.

Ant. The duke cannot deny the course of law,

For the commodity that strangers have

With us in Venice, if it be denied,

'Twill much impeach the justice of the state;

Since that the trade and profit of the city

Consisteth of all nations.

Well, gaoler, on:—Pray heaven, Bassanio come

To see me pay his debt, and then I care not.

Exeunt.

SCENE V.—SALOON OF THE CASKETS IN PORTIA'S HOUSE AT BELMONT.

Enter PORTIA, NERISSA, LORENZO, JESSICA, and BALTHAZAR.

Lor. Madam, although I speak it in your presence,

You have a noble and a true conceit

Of god-like amity; which appears most strongly

In bearing thus the absence of your lord.

But, if you knew to whom you show this honour,

How true a gentleman you send relief,

How dear a lover of my lord your husband,

I know you would be prouder of the work,

Than customary bounty can enforce you.

Por. I never did repent for doing good,

Nor shall not now.

This comes too near the praising of myself;

Therefore, no more of it: hear other things.

Lorenzo, I commit into your hands

The husbandry and manage of my house,
Until my lord's return: for mine own part,
I have toward heaven breath'd a secret vow,
To live in prayer and contemplation,
Only attended by Nerissa here;
There is a monastery two miles off,
And there we will abide. I do desire you
Not to deny this imposition;
To which my love, and some necessity,
Now lays upon you.
Lor. Madam, with all my heart,
I shall obey you in all fair commands.
Por. My people do already know my mind,
And will acknowledge you and Jessica
In place of lord Bassanio and myself.
So fare you well, till we shall meet again.
Lor. Fair thoughts and happy hours attend on you!
Jes. I wish your ladyship all heart's content.
Por. I thank you for your wish, and am well pleas'd
To wish it back on you: fare you well, Jessica!
Exeunt JESSICA and LORENZO.
Now, Balthazar,
As I have ever found thee honest, true,
So let me find thee still: Take this same letter;
See thou render this
Into my cousin's hand, doctor Bellario;
And, look, what notes and garments he doth give thee

Bring them, I pray thee, with imagin'd speed

Unto the tranect, to the common ferry

Which trades to Venice:—waste no time in words,

But get thee gone; I shall be there before thee.

Bal. Madam, I go with all convenient speed.

Exit.

Por. Come on, Nerissa; I have work in hand,

That you yet know not of: we'll see our husbands,

Before they think of us.

Ner. Shall they see us?

Por. They shall, Nerissa:

But come, I'll tell thee all my whole device

When I am in my coach, which stays for us

At the park gate; and therefore haste away,

For we must measure twenty miles to-day.

Exeunt.

END OF ACT THIRD.

ACT IV.

SCENE I.—VENICE. A COURT OF JUSTICE.

The DUKE, the MAGNIFICOES ANTONIO, BASSANIO, GRATIANO, SALARINO, SALANIO, and others.

Duke. What is Antonio here?

Ant. Ready, so please your grace.

Duke, I am sorry for thee: them art come to answer

A stony adversary, an inhuman wretch,

Uncapable of pity, void and empty

From any dram of mercy.

Ant. I have heard

Your grace hath ta'en great pains to qualify

His rigorous course; but since he stands obdurate,

And that no lawful means can carry me

Out of his envy's reach, I do oppose

My patience to his fury; and am arm'd

To suffer, with a quietness of spirit,

The very tyranny and rage of his.

Duke. Go one, and call the Jew into the court.

Grand Capt. He's ready at the door: he comes, my lord.

Enter SHYLOCK.

Duke. Make room, and let him stand before our face.

Shylock, the world thinks, and I think so, too,

That thou but lead'st this fashion of thy malice

To the last hour of act: and then, 'tis thought

Thou'lt show thy mercy and remorse, more strange

Than is thy strange apparent cruelty:

And where thou now exact'st the penalty,

(Which is a pound of this poor merchant's flesh),

Thou wilt not only lose the forfeiture,

But touch'd with human gentleness and love,

Forgive a moiety of the principal;

Glancing an eye of pity on his losses,

That have of late so huddled on his back,

Enough to press a royal merchant down,

And pluck commiseration of his state

From brassy bosoms, and rough hearts of flint,
From stubborn Turks and Tartars, never train'd
To offices of tender courtesy.
We all expect a gentle answer, Jew.
Shy. I have possess'd your grace of what I purpose;
And by our holy Sabbath have I sworn,
To have the due and forfeit of my bond:
If you deny it, let the danger light
Upon your charter, and your city's freedom.
You'll ask me, why I rather choose to have
A weight of carrion flesh, than to receive
Three thousand ducats: I'll not answer that:
But, say, it is my humour: Is it answer'd?
What if my house be troubled with a rat,
And I be pleas'd to give ten thousand ducats
To have it ban'd? What, are you answer'd yet?
Some men there are love not a gaping pig;
Some, that are mad if they behold a cat;
Now for your answer.
As there is no firm reason to be render'd
Why he cannot abide a gaping pig;
Why he a harmless necessary cat;
So can I give no reason, nor I will not,
More than a lodg'd hate, and a certain loathing,
I bear Antonio, that I follow thus
A losing suit against him. Are you answer'd?
Bas. This is no answer, thou unfeeling man,

To excuse the current of thy cruelty.
Shy. I am not bound to please thee with my answer.
Bas. Do all men kill the things they do not love?
Shy. Hates any man the thing he would not kill?
Bas. Every offence is not a hate at first.
Shy. What, would'st thou have a serpent sting thee twice?
Ant. I pray you, think you question with the Jew.
You may as well go stand upon the beach,
And bid the main flood bate his usual height;
Yon may as well use question with the wolf,
Why he hath made the ewe bleat for the lamb;
You may as well forbid the mountain pines
To wag their high tops, and to make no noise,
When they are fretted with the gusts of heaven;
You may as well do anything most hard,
As seek to soften that (than which what's harder?)
His Jewish heart:—Therefore, I do beseech you,
Make no more offers, use no further means,
But, with all brief and plain conveniency,
Let me have judgment, and the Jew his will.
Bas. For thy three thousand ducats here are six.
Shy. If every ducat in six thousand ducats
Were in six parts, and every part a ducat,
I would not draw them,—I would have my bond.
Duke. How shall thou hope for mercy, rend'ring none?
Shy. What judgment shall I dread, doing no wrong?
You have among you many a purchas'd slave,

Which, like your asses, and your dogs, and mules,
You use in abject and in slavish parts,
Because you bought them:—Shall I say to you,
Let them be free, marry them to your heirs?
Why sweat they under burthens? let their beds
Be made as soft as yours, and let their palates
Be season'd with such viands? You will answer,
The slaves are ours:—So do I answer you.
The pound of flesh, which I demand of him.
Is dearly bought; 'tis mine, and I will have it;
If you deny me, fie upon your law!
There is no force in the decrees of Venice:
I stand for judgment: answer; shall I have it?
Duke. Upon my power, I may dismiss this court,
Unless Bellario, a learned doctor,
Whom I have sent for to determine this,
Come here to day.
Grand Capt. My lord, here stays without
A messenger, with letters from the doctor,
New come from Padua.
Duke. Bring us the letters:—Call the messenger.
Bas. Good cheer, Antonio! What, man! courage yet!
The Jew shall have my flesh, blood, bones, and all,
Ere thou shall lose for me one drop of blood.
Ant. I am a tainted wether of the flock,
Meetest for death; the weakest kind of fruit
Drops earliest to the ground, and so let me:

You cannot better be employ'd, Bassanio,

Than to live still, and write mine epitaph.

Enter NERISSA, dressed like a lawyer's clerk.

Duke. Came you from Padua, from Bellario?

Ner. From both, my lord; Bellario greets your grace.

Presents a letter.

Bas. Why dost thou whet thy knife so earnestly?

Shy. To cut the forfeit from that bankrupt there.

Gra. Can no prayers pierce thee?

Shy. No, none that thou hast wit enough to make.

Gra. O, be thou damn'd inexorable dog!

And for thy life let justice be accus'd.

Thou almost makst me waver in my faith,

To hold opinion with Pythagoras,

That souls of animals infuse themselves

Into the trunks of men: thy currish spirit

Govern'd a wolf, who, hang'd for human slaughter,

Even from the gallows did his fell soul fleet,

And whilst thou lay'st in thy unhallow'd dam,

Infus'd itself in thee; for thy desires

Are wolfish, bloody, starv'd, and ravenous.

Shy. Till thou can'st rail the seal from off my bond,

Thou but offend'st thy lungs to speak so loud:

Repair thy wit, good youth; or it will fall

To cureless ruin.—I stand here for law.

Duke. This letter from Bellario doth commend

A young and learned doctor tax our court:—

Where is he?

Ner. He attendeth here hard by,

To know your answer, whether you'll admit him.

Duke. With all my heart:—some three or four of you

Go give him courteous conduct to this place.—

Meantime, the court shall hear Bellario's letter.

Herald reads] "Your grace shall understand, that, at the receipt of your letter, I am very sick; but that in the instant that your messenger came, in loving visitation was with me a young doctor of Home; his name is Balthasar: I acquainted him with the cause in controversy between the Jew and Antonio, the merchant: we turned o'er many books together; he is furnished with my opinion; which, better'd with his own learning (the greatness whereof I cannot enough commend), comes with him, at my importunity, to fill up your grace's request in my stead. I beseech you, let his lack of years be no impediment to let him lack a reverend estimation; for I never knew so young a body with so old a head. I leave him to your gracious acceptance, whose trial shall better publish his commendation."

Duke. You hear the learn'd Bellario, what he writes:

And here, I take it, is the doctor come.

Enter PORTIA, dressed like a Doctor of Laws.

Give me your hand: Came you from old Bellario?

Por. I did, my lord.

Duke. You are welcome: take your place.

Are you acquainted with the difference

That holds this present question in the court?

Por. I am informed throughly of the cause.

Which is the merchant here, and which the Jew?

Duke. Antonio and old Shylock, both stand forth.

Por. Is your name Shylock?

Shy. Shylock is my name.

Por. Of a strange nature is the suit you follow;

Yet in such rule that the Venetian law

Cannot impugn you, as you do proceed.—You

stand within his danger, do you not?

To ANTONIO.

Ant. Ay, so he says.

Por. So you confess the bond?

Ant. I do.

Por. Then must the Jew be merciful.

Shy. On what compulsion must I? Tell me that.

Por. The quality of mercy is not strain'd;

It droppeth, as the gentle rain from heaven

Upon the place beneath: it is twice bless'd;

It blesseth him that gives, and him that takes;

'Tis mightiest in the mightiest: it becomes

The throned monarch better than his crown;

His sceptre shows the force of temporal power,

The attribute to awe and majesty,

Wherein doth sit the dread and fear of kings;

But mercy is above this sceptred sway,

It is enthroned in the hearts of kings,

It is an attribute to God himself;

And earthly power doth then show likest God's

When mercy seasons justice. Therefore, Jew,

Though justice be thy plea, consider this—That

in the course of justice, none of us

Should see salvation: we do pray for mercy;

And that same prayer doth teach us all to render

The deeds of mercy. I have spoke thus much,
To mitigate the justice of thy plea;
Which if thou follow, this strict court of Venice
Must needs give sentence 'gainst the merchant there.
Shy., My deeds upon my head! I crave the law,
The penalty and forfeit of my bond.
Por. Is he not able to discharge the money?
Bas. Yes, here I tender it for him in the court;
Yea, thrice the sum: if that will not suffice,
I will be bound to pay it ten times o'er,
On forfeit of my hands, my head, my heart:
If this will not suffice, it must appear
That malice bears down truth. And I beseech you,
Wrest once the law to your authority:
To do a great right to do a little wrong;
And curb this cruel devil of his will.
Por. It must not be; there is no power in Venice
Can alter a decree established:
'Twill be recorded for a precedent;
And many an error, by the same example,
Will rush into the state; it cannot be.
Shy. A Daniel come to judgment! yea, a Daniel!
O wise young judge, how do I honour thee!
Por. I pray you, let me look upon the bond.
Shy. Here 'tis, most reverend doctor, here it is.
Por. Shylock, there's thrice thy money offer'd thee.
Shy. An oath, an oath, I have an oath in heaven:

Shall I lay perjury upon my soul?
No, not for Venice.
Por. Why, this bond is forfeit;
And lawfully by this the Jew may claim
A pound of flesh, to be by him cut off
Nearest the merchant's heart:—Be merciful;
Take thrice thy money; bid me tear the bond.
Shy. When it is paid according to the tenour.
It doth appear you are a worthy judge;
You know the law, your exposition
Hath been most sound: I charge you by the law,
Whereof you are a well-deserving pillar,
Proceed to judgment: by my soul I swear,
There is no power in the tongue of man
To alter me: I stay here on my bond.
Ant. Most heartily I do beseech the court
To give the judgment.
Por. Why then, thus it is:
You must prepare your bosom for his knife.
Shy. O noble judge! O excellent young man!
Por. For the intent and purpose of the law
Hath full relation to the penalty,
Which here appeareth due upon the bond.
Shy. 'Tis very true: O wise and upright judge!
How much more elder art thou than thy looks!
Por. Therefore, lay bare your bosom.
Shy. Ay, his breast:

So says the bond;—Doth it not, noble judge?—Nearest his heart, those are the very words.

Por. It is so. Are there balance here to weigh

The flesh?

Shy. I have them ready.

Por. Have by some surgeon, Shylock, on your charge,

To stop his wounds, lest he should bleed to death.

Shy. Is it so nominated in the bond?

Por. It is not so express'd; but what of that?

'Twere good you do so much for charity.

Shy. I cannot find it; 'tis not in the bond.

Por. Come, merchant, have you anything to say?

Ant. But little; I am arm'd and well prepar'd.—

Give me your hand, Bassanio; fare you well!

Grieve not that I am fallen to this for you;

For herein fortune shows herself more kind

Than is her custom: it is still her use,

To let the wretched man outlive his wealth,

To view with hollow eye and wrinkled brow,

An age of poverty: from which lingering penance

Of such a misery doth she cut me off.

Commend me to your honorable wife:

Tell her the process of Antonio's end;

Say, how I lov'd you, speak me fair in death;

And, when the tale is told, bid her be judge

Whether Bassanio had not once a love.

Repent not you that you shall lose your friend,

And he repents not that he pays your debt;

For, if the Jew do cut but deep enough,

I'll pay it instantly with all my heart.

Bas. Antonio, I am married to a wife,

Which is as dear to me as life itself;

But life itself, my wife, and all the world,

Are not with me esteem'd above thy life;

I would lose all, ay, sacrifice them all

Here to this devil, to deliver you.

Gra. I have a wife, whom I protest I love;

I would she were in heaven, so she could

Entreat some power to change this currish Jew.

Shy. These be the Christian husbands: I have a daughter;

Would any of the stock of Barrabas

Had been her husband, rather than a Christian! Aside.

We trifle time; I pray thee pursue sentence.

Por. A pound of that same merchant's flesh is thine;

The court awards it, and the law doth give it.

Shy. Most rightful judge!

Por. And you must cut this flesh from off his breast!

The law allows it, and the court awards it.

Shy. Most learned judge!—A sentence; come, prepare.

Por. Tarry a little;—there is something else.—

This bond doth give thee here no jot of blood;

The words expressly are a pound of flesh:

Then take thy bond, take thou thy pound of flesh;

But, in the cutting it, if thou dost shed

One drop of Christian blood, thy lands and goods
Are, by the laws of Venice, confiscate
Unto the state of Venice.
Gra. O upright judge!—Mark, Jew!—O learned judge!
Shy. Is that the law?
Por. Thyself shall see the act;
For, as thou urgest justice, be assur'd
Thou shalt have justice more than thou desir'st.
Gra. O learned judge!—Mark Jew;—a learned judge!
Shy. I take his offer, then,—pay the bond thrice,
And let the Christian go.
Bas. Here is the money.
Por. Soft.
The Jew shall have all justice;—soft;—no haste;—He
shall have nothing but the penalty.
Gra. O Jew! an upright judge, a learned judge!
Por. Therefore, prepare thee to cut off the flesh.
Shed thou no blood; nor cut thou less, nor more,
But just a pound of flesh: if thou tak'st more,
Or less, than a just pound,—be it but so much
As makes it light or heavy in the balance,
Or the division of the twentieth part
Of one poor scruple,—nay, if the scale do turn
But in the estimation of a hair,—
Thou diest, and all thy goods are confiscate.
Gra. A second Daniel, a Daniel, Jew!
Now, infidel, I have thee on the hip.

Por. Why doth the Jew pause? take thy forfeiture.

Shy. Give me my principal, and let me go.

Bas. I have it ready for thee; here it is.

Por. He hath refus'd it in the open court;

He shall have merely justice, and his bond.

Gra. A Daniel, still say I; a second Daniel!—

thank thee, Jew, for teaching me that word.

Shy. Shall I not barely have my principal?

Por. Thou shalt have nothing but the forfeiture,

To be so taken at thy peril, Jew.

Shy. Why then the devil give him good of it!

I'll stay no longer question.

Por. Tarry, Jew;

The law hath yet another hold on you.

It is enacted in the laws of Venice,—If

it be proved against an alien,

That by direct or indirect attempts

He seek the life of any citizen,

The party 'gainst the which he doth contrive

Shall seize one half his goods; the other half

Comes to the privy coffer of the state;

And the offender's life lies in the mercy

Of the duke only, 'gainst all other voice.

In which predicament, I say, thou stand'st:

For it appears by manifest proceeding,

That, indirectly, and directly, too,

Thou hast contriv'd against the very life

Of the defendant; and thou hast incurr'd
The danger formerly by me rehears'd.
Down, therefore, and beg mercy of the duke.
Gra. Beg that thou may'st have leave to hang thyself:
And yet, thy wealth being forfeit to the state,
Thou hast not left the value of a cord;
Therefore, thou must be hang'd at the state's charge.
Duke. That thou shall see the difference of our spirit,
I pardon thee thy life before thou ask it:
For half thy wealth, it is Antonio's;
The other half comes to the general state,
Which humbleness may drive unto a fine.
Por. Ay, for the state; not for Antonio.
Shy. Nay, take my life and all, pardon not that:
You take my house, when you do take the prop
That doth sustain my house; you take my life,
When you do take the means whereby I live.
Por. What mercy can you render him, Antonio?
Gra. A halter gratis; nothing else, for Heaven's sake.
Ant. So please my lord the duke, and all the court,
To quit the fine for one half of his goods;
I am content, so he will let me have
The other half in use, to render it,
Upon his death, unto the gentleman
That lately stole his daughter;
Two things provided more,—That for this favour,
He presently become a Christian;

The other, that he do record a gift,

Here in the court, of all he dies possess'd,

Unto his son Lorenzo and his daughter.

Duke. He shall do this; or else I do recant

The pardon that I late pronounced here.

Por. Art thou contented, Jew? What dost thou say?

Shy. I am content.

Por. Clerk, draw a deed of gift.

Shy. I pray you give me leave to go from hence:

I am not well; send the deed after me,

And I will sign it.

Duke. Get thee gone, but do it.

Gra. In christening; thou shalt have two godfathers;

Had I been judge, thou should'st have had ten more,

To bring thee to the gallows, not to the font.

Exit SHYLOCK.

Duke. Sir, I entreat you with me home to dinner.

Por. I humbly do desire your grace of pardon.

I must away this night toward Padua;

And it is meet I presently set forth.

Duke. I am sorry that your leisure serves you not:

Antonio, gratify this gentleman;

For, in my mind, you are much bound to him.

Exeunt DUKE, Magnificoes, and Train.

Bas. Most worthy gentleman, I and my friend,

Have by your wisdom been this day acquitted

Of grievous penalties; in lieu whereof,

Three thousand ducats, due unto the Jew,
We freely cope your courteous pains withal.
Ant. And stand indebted, over and above,
In love and service to you evermore.
Por. He is well paid that is well satisfied:
And I, delivering you, am satisfied,
And therein do account myself well paid;
My mind was never yet more mercenary.
I pray you know me, when we meet again;
I wish you well, and so I take my leave.
Bas. Dear Sir, of force I must attempt you further;
Take some remembrance of us, as a tribute,
Not as a fee: grant me two things, I pray you,
Not to deny me, and to pardon me.
Por. You press me far, and therefore I will yield,
Give me your gloves, I'll wear them for your sake;
And, for your love, I'll take this ring from you:—Do
not draw back your hand; I'll take no more;
And you in love shall not deny me this.
Bas. This ring, good Sir,—alas, it is a trifle;
I will not shame myself to give you this.
Por. I will have nothing else but only this;
And now, methinks, I have a mind to it.
Bas. There's more depends on this than on the value.
The dearest ring in Venice will I give you,
And find it out by proclamation;
Only for this I pray you pardon me.

Por. I see, Sir, you are liberal in offers:

You taught me first to beg; and now, methinks,

You teach me how a beggar should be answer'd.

Bas. Good Sir, this ring was given me by my wife;

And when she put it on, she made me vow

That I should neither sell, nor give, nor lose it.

Por. That 'scuse serves many men to save their gifts.

An if your wife be not a mad woman,

And know how well I have deserv'd this ring,

She would not hold out enemy for ever,

For giving it to me. Well, peace be with you!

Exeunt PORTIA and NERISSA.

Ant. My lord Bassanio, let him have the ring;

Let his deservings, and my love withal,

Be valued 'gainst your wife's commandment.

Bas. Go, Gratiano, run and overtake him;

Give him the ring; and bring him, if thou can'st,

Unto Antonio's house;—away, make haste.

Exit GRATIANO.

Come, you and I will thither presently;

And in the morning early will we both

Fly toward Belmont: Come, Antonio.

Exeunt.

SCENE II.—VENICE. THE FOSCARI GATE OF THE DUCAL PALACE, LEADING TO THE GIANT'S STAIRCASE.

Enter PORTIA and NERISSA.

Por. Inquire the Jew's house out, give him this deed, And let him sign it; we'll away to-night, And be a day before our husbands home: This deed will be well welcome to Lorenzo.

Enter GRATIANO.

Gra. Fair Sir, you are well overtaken: My lord Bassanio, upon more advice, Hath sent you here this ring; and doth entreat Your company at dinner.

Por. That cannot be: This ring I do accept most thankfully, And so, I pray you, tell him: Furthermore, I pray you, show my youth old Shylock's house.

Gra. That will I do.

Ner. Sir, I would speak with you:—I'll see if I can get my husband's ring,

To PORTIA.

Which I did make him swear to keep for ever.

Por. Thou may'st, I warrant. We shall have old swearing, That they did give the rings away to men; But we'll outface them, and outswear them, too. Away, make haste; thou know'st where I will tarry.

Ner. Come, good Sir, will you show me to this house?

Exeunt.

END OF ACT FOURTH.

ACT V.

SCENE I.—BELMONT. AVENUE TO PORTIA'S HOUSE.

Enter LORENZO and JESSICA.

Lor. The moon shines bright:—In such a night as this,

When the sweet wind did gently kiss the trees,

And they did make no noise,—in such a night,

Troilus, methinks, mounted the Trojan walls,

And sigh'd his soul toward the Grecian tents,

Where Cressid lay that night.

Jes. In such a night

Bid young Lorenzo swear he lov'd me well;

Stealing my soul with many vows of faith,

And ne'er a true one.

Lor. In such a night,

Did pretty Jessica, like a little shrew,

Slander her love, and he forgave it her.

Jes. I would out-night you, did no body come:

But, hark, I hear the footing of a man.

Enter BALTHAZAR.

Lor. Who comes so fast in silence of the night?

Bal. A friend,

Lor. A friend? what friend? your name, I pray you,

friend.

Bal. Balthazar is my name: and I bring word,

My mistress will before the break of day

Be here at Belmont.

I pray you, is my master yet return'd?

Lor. He is not, nor we have not heard from him.—

But go we in, I pray thee, Jessica,

And ceremoniously let us prepare

Some welcome for the mistress of the house.

Enter LANCELOT.

Lau. Sola, sola, we ha, ho, sola, sola.

Lor. Who calls?

Lau. Sola! Did you see master Lorenzo, and mistress Lorenzo? sola, sola

Lor. Leave holloing, man; here.

Lau. Sola! where? where?

Lor. Here.

Lau. Tell him, there's a post come from my master, with his horn full of good news; my master will be here ere morning.

Exit.

Lor. My friend Balthazar, signify, I pray you,

Within the house, your mistress is at hand:

And bring your music forth into the air. Exit BALTHAZAR.

How sweet the moon-light sleeps upon this bank!

Here will we sit, and let the sounds of music

Creep in our ears: soft stillness, and the night,

Become the touches of sweet harmony.

Sit, Jessica. Look how the floor of heaven

Is thick inlaid with patines of bright gold.

There's not the smallest orb which thou behold'st

But in his motion like an angel sings,

Still quiring to the young-eyed cherubins:

Such harmony is in immortal souls,

But whilst this muddy vesture of decay

Doth grossly close it in, we cannot hear it.—

Enter MUSICIANS.

GLEE.

It was a lover and his lass,With a hey and a ho, and a hey nonino;That o'er the green corn fields did pass,In the spring-time, the pretty spring time,When birds do sing, hey ding-a-ding, ding:—Sweet lovers love the spring.

And therefore take the present time,With a hey and a ho, and a hey nonino;For love is crowned with the primeIn the spring-time, the pretty spring time,When birds do sing, hey ding-a-ding, ding:—Sweet lovers love the spring.

Jes. I am never merry when I hear sweet music.

Lor. The reason is your spirits are attentive:

For do but note a wild and wanton herd,
If any air of music touch their ears,
You shall perceive them make a mutual stand,
Their savage eyes turn'd to a modest gaze,
By the sweet power of music. Therefore, the poet
Did feign that Orpheus drew trees, stones, and floods;
Since nought so stockish, hard, and full of rage,
But music for the time doth change his nature:
The man that hath no music in himself,
Nor is not mov'd with concord of sweet sounds,
Is fit for treasons, stratagems, and spoils;
The motions of his spirit are dull as night,
And his affections dark as Erebus:
Let no such man be trusted.—Mark the music.

Enter PORTIA and NERISSA, at a distance.

Por. That light we see is burning in my hall.
How far that little candle throws his beams!
So shines a good deed in a naughty world. Music! hark!

Ner. It is your music, madam, of the house.

Por. Nothing is good, I see, without respect;
Methinks it sounds much sweeter than by day.

Ner. Silence bestows that virtue on it, madam.

Music ceases.

Por. How many things by season season'd are
To their light praise, and true-perfection!—

Lor. That is the voice,
Or I am much deceiv'd, of Portia.

Por. He knows me, as the blind man knows the cuckoo,

By the bad voice.

Lor. Dear lady, welcome home.

Por. We have been praying for our husbands' welfare,

Which speed, we hope, the better for our words.

Are they return'd?

Lor. Madam, they are not yet;

But there is come a messenger before,

To signify their coming.

Por. Go in, Nerissa;

Give order to my servants, that they take

No note at all of our being absent hence;

Nor you, Lorenzo;—Jessica, nor you.

A trumpet sounds.

Lor. Your husband is at hand; I hear his trumpet:

We are no tell-tales, madam; fear you not.

Enter BASSANIO, ANTONIO, GRATIANO, and their Followers.

Por. You are welcome home, my lord.

Bas. I thank you, madam: give welcome to my friend.—

This is the man, this is Antonio,

To whom I am so infinitely bound.

Por. You should in all sense be much bound to him,

For, as I hear, he was much bound for you.

Ant. No more than I am well acquitted of.

Por. Sir, you are very welcome to our house:

It must appear in other ways than words,

Therefore, I scant this breathing courtesy.

GRATIANO and NERISSA seem to talk apart.

Gra. By yonder moon, I swear you do me wrong;

In faith, I gave it to the judge's clerk:

Would he were hang'd that had it, for my part,

Since you do take it, love, so much at heart.

Por. A quarrel, ho, already? What's the matter?

Gra. About a hoop of gold, a paltry ring

That she did give to me; whose posy was

For all the world, like cutler's poetry

Upon a knife, 'Love me, and leave me not.'

Ner. What talk you of the posy, or the value?

You swore to me, when I did give it you,

That you would wear it till the hour of death:

And that it should lie with you in your grave;

Though not for me, yet for your vehement oaths,

You should have been respective, and have kept it.

Gave it a judge's clerk!—but well I know,

The clerk will ne'er wear hair on's face that had it.

Gra. He will, an if he live to be a man.

Ner. Ay, if a woman live to be a man.

Gra. Now, by this hand, I gave it to a youth,—

kind of boy; a little scrubbed boy,

No higher than thyself, the judge's clerk;

A prating boy, that begg'd it as a fee;

I could not for my heart deny it him.

Por. You were to blame, I must be plain with you,

To part so slightly with your wife's first gift:

A thing stuck on with oaths upon your finger,
And so riveted with faith unto your flesh.
I gave my love a ring, and made him swear
Never to part with it; and here he stands,—
I dare be sworn for him, he would not leave it,
Nor pluck it from his finger, for the wealth
That the world masters. Now, in faith, Gratiano,
You give your wife too unkind a cause of grief;
An 'twere to me, I should be mad at it.
Bas. Why, I were best to cut my left hand off,
And swear, I lost the ring defending it.
Aside.
Gra. My lord Bassanio gave his ring away
Unto the judge that begg'd it, and, indeed,
Deserv'd it, too; and then the boy, his clerk,
That took some pains in writing, he begg'd mine:
And neither man, nor master, would take aught
But the two rings.
Por. What ring gave you, my lord;
Not that, I hope, which you receiv'd of me.
Bas. If I could add a lie unto a fault,
I would deny it; but you see, my finger
Hath not the ring upon it, it is gone.
Por. Even so void is your false heart of truth.
By heaven, I will ne'er come in your sight
Until I see the ring.
Ner. Nor I in yours,

Till I again see mine.

Bas. Sweet Portia,

If you did know to whom I gave the ring,

If you did know for whom I gave the ring,

And would conceive for what I gave the ring,

And how unwillingly I left the ring,

When nought would be accepted but the ring,

You would abate the strength of your displeasure.

Por. If you had known the virtue of the ring,

Or half her worthiness that gave the ring,

Or your own honour to contain the ring,

You would not then have parted with the ring.

What man is there so much unreasonable,

If you had pleas'd to have defended it

With any terms of zeal, wanted the modesty

To urge the thing held as a ceremony?

Nerissa teaches me what to believe;

I'll die for't, but some woman had the ring.

Bas. No, by mine honour, madam, by my soul,

No woman had it, but a civil doctor,

Which did refuse three thousand ducats of me,

And begg'd the ring; the which I did deny him,

And suffer'd him to go displeas'd away;

Even he that had held up the very life

Of my dear friend. What should I say, sweet lady?

I was enforc'd to send it after him.

Had you been there, I think you would have begg'd

The ring of me to give the worthy doctor.

Por. Let not that doctor e'er come near my house:

Since he hath got the jewel that I lov'd,

And that which you did swear to keep for me,

I will become as liberal as you.

Ant. I am the unhappy subject of these quarrels.

Por. Sir, grieve not you; you are welcome notwithstanding.

Bas. Portia, forgive me this enforced wrong;

And in the hearing of these many friends,

I swear to thee, even by thine own fair eyes,

I never more will break an oath with thee.

Ant. I once did lend my body for his wealth;

Which, but for him that had your husband's ring,

To PORTIA.

Had quite miscarried: I dare be bound again,

My soul upon the forfeit, that your lord

Will never more break faith advisedly.

Por. Then you shall be his surety: give him this;

And bid him keep it better than the other.

Ant. Here, lord Bassanio; swear to keep this ring.

Bas. By heaven it is the same I gave the doctor!

Por. I had it of him: pardon me, Bassanio.

Ner. And pardon me, my gentle Gratiano;

For that same scrubbed boy, the doctor's clerk,

Did give me this.

Gra. Why this is like the mending of highways

In summer, when the ways are fair enough.

Por. You are all amaz'd:

Here is a letter, read it at your leisure;

It comes from Padua, from Bellario:

There you shall find, that Portia was the doctor;

Nerissa there, her clerk: Lorenzo here

Shall witness, I set forth as soon as you,

And but e'en now return'd; I have not yet

Enter'd my house.—Antonio, you are welcome;

And I have better news in store for you

Than you expect: unseal this letter soon,

There you shall find three of your argosies

Are richly come to harbour suddenly:

You shall not know by what strange accident

I chanced on this letter.

Bas. Were you the doctor, and I knew you not?

Gra. Were you the clerk, and I knew you not?

Ant. Sweet lady, you have given me life, and living;

For here I read for certain, that my ships

Are safely come to road.

Por. How now, Lorenzo?

My clerk has some good comforts too for you.

Ner. Ay, and I'll give them him without a fee.—

There do I give to you Jessica,

From the rich Jew a special deed of gift,

After his death, of all he dies possessed of.

Lor. Fair ladies, you drop manna in the way of starved people.

Por. It is almost morning,

And yet I am sure you are not satisfied

Of these events at full: Let us go in;

And charge us there upon inter'gatories,

And we will answer all things faithfully.

Exeunt.

Gra. Let it be so, the first intergatory
That my Nerrissa shall be sworne on, is,
Whether till the next night she had rather stay,
Or goe to bed, now being two houres to day,
But were the day come, I should wish it darke,
Till I were couching with the Doctors Clarke.
Well, while I liue, Ile feare no other thing
So sore, as keeping safe Nerrissas ring.

Exeunt.

FINIS. The Merchant of Venice.

THE END

www.ingramcontent.com/pod-product-compliance
Lightning Source LLC
La Vergne TN
LVHW101929220826
846093LV00009B/407

* 9 7 8 2 3 8 2 7 4 6 7 0 7 *